REACHING FOR THE STARS

TOM HANKS
Academy Award-Winning Actor

Rosemary Wallner

Published by Abdo & Daughters, 4940 Viking Drive, Suite 622, Edina, Minnesota 55435.

Library bound edition distributed by Rockbottom Books, Pentagon Tower, P.O. Box 36036, Minneapolis, Minnesota 55435.

Printed in the United States.

Cover Photo credit: Shooting Star
Interior Photo credits: Shooting Star

Edited by Bob Italia

LIBRARY OF CONGRESS CATALOGING-IN-PUBLICATION DATA

Wallner, Rosemary, 1964—
    Tom Hanks / Rosemary Wallner.
          p.   cm. -- (Reaching for the stars)
    ISBN 1-56239-338-3
    1. Hanks, Tom -- Juvenile literature. 2. Motion picture actors and actresses -- United States --Biography -- Juvenile literature.
    [1. Hanks, Tom, 2. Actors and actresses.] I. Title. II. Series.
    PN2287.H18W35   1994
    [B]   94-22191
                                                                 CIP
                                                                 AC

TABLE OF CONTENTS

OUTGOING, VERBAL, AND QUIRKY

Reporters have been interviewing Tom Hanks ever since he began appearing in movies in the 1980s. Here's how some of them have described this talented actor:

"Bright, outgoing, verbal." —*Newsweek* magazine

"Average guy, down to earth, kind of quirky." —*Vogue* magazine

"Hanks doesn't walk around with a sign that says love me; he doesn't have to." —*People* magazine

In the first five years of his movie career, Hanks appeared in 13 movies. The movies included the hits *Splash*, *Nothing in Common*, *Punchline*, and *Big*. After a short rest, Hanks began acting again. In the next five years of his career, he appeared in five more movies. Those films included *Sleepless in Seattle* and *Philadelphia*.

"I've made so many movies. It's as though I was on a mission to have one of my movies playing in every other theater in America," said Hanks about his hectic work schedule.

What does Hanks feel about all the publicity and fame he's found since his first movie roles? In a 1993 interview he told one reporter, "...I feel like there's nothing special about me just because I'm the current guy in a good movie."

Despite what Hanks might feel, his fans think there's something special about him. And they can't wait for his next movie—and his next interview.

A CHILDHOOD SPENT ON THE MOVE

Thomas J. Hanks was born on July 9, 1956, in Concord, California. He lived in this town just north of San Francisco with his parents, an older brother and sister, and a younger brother. Hanks's father worked at different jobs in the restaurant business. Hanks's mother was a waitress.

When he was five years old, Hanks's mother and father divorced. Mr. Hanks packed his car with his belongings and took Hanks and his older brother and sister. His mother stayed in Concord with Hanks's six-month-old brother.

As Hanks grew up, his father changed jobs often. With each new job came a move to a new home. Most of the moves were to cities up and down the California coast. "I moved about a million times," remarked Hanks. "We moved every six months of my life."

When Mr. Hanks married a woman with five children, Hanks and his siblings moved to a larger home. When that marriage ended in divorce, it meant another move. Even as a young child, however, Hanks liked the adventure of moving to different cities.

"We lived in so many places," Hanks said, "there was a dazzling array of sets to play on."

By the time he was ten years old, Hanks had had three mothers, attended five grammar schools, and lived in ten houses.

When Hanks remembers all the moving around, he was glad he could count on his older brother and sister. They were the people he was around most—he saw them more than he saw his parents.

At first Hanks's family didn't think of him as a funny guy. In fact, Hanks remembered that his family thought his older brother, Larry, was the funniest brother. "People used to say, 'Tom's loud,'" recalled Hanks. "And then they'd say, 'But Larry—now *Larry's* funny.'"

His family's description of him didn't bother Hanks too much because he could always be funny in school. "In school," he revealed, "I was the guy who could always come up with funny quotes for whatever slides they were showing in class." Although he was shy, he used humor to make friends with kids in all the schools he went to.

When Hanks was in junior high, his father met and married his third wife. With this new marriage, Mr. Hanks was ready to settle down. He moved the family one more time to Oakland Hills near Berkeley, California. Hanks and his brother and sister were also ready to stay in one place.

Once Hanks was settled in Oakland Hills, Hanks became interested in outer space. He began spending all his time at the Oakland Public School Planetarium. He also became interested in movies.

He watched the space movie *2001: A Space Odyssey* 22 times. Whenever he could, he watched movies on TV and in the theaters.

Once Hanks started high school, he discovered drama class. He acted in a few school plays, but, as Hanks remembered, he had other interests as well. He was a member of the track team and was named class clown in his yearbook. When he graduated from high school in 1974, he enrolled in a Bay area junior college. He wasn't sure what career he would choose. He was open to exploring just about anything.

CHOOSING A CAREER

After two years of classes at the junior college, Hanks was getting restless. What field did he want to learn more about? What kind of job did he want? He knew he was a fun person. He knew he was someone who could think fast on his feet. He knew he was still a loud person, just as his family had said years ago. As he looked for answers, he began to think about an acting career.

"Acting class looked like the best place for a guy who liked to make a lot of noise and be rather flamboyant," Hanks declared. Once he had decided on what to study, he felt better about himself. He transferred to California State University in Sacramento. He began appearing in plays. He worked hard behind the scenes at the college theater. He worked the lighting board. He learned how to become a stage manager.

He also began to study other actors. "I spent a lot of time going to plays," said Hanks. "I wouldn't take dates with me. I'd just drive to a theater, buy myself a ticket, sit in the seat and read the program, and then get into the play completely."

In his third year of college, Hanks auditioned for a college play but was not chosen as a cast member. Because he wanted to act in something, he auditioned for a community play and earned a small part. There, he met Vincent Dowling, the guest director.

Dowling knew that Hanks had something special. "Tom's magic as an actor comes from an abundance of life," Dowling once said. "Tom was always happiest on stage, even at 18." One of Dowling's jobs was to manage the Great Lakes Theater Festival in Cleveland, Ohio. He needed actors to help him with his next season of plays. When the community play ended, Dowling asked Hanks to move to Cleveland for a year. Hanks agreed.

Once in Cleveland, Hanks helped out wherever he could. He wanted to learn everything about acting. He worked as a carpenter, stage manager, and set designer. He painted backdrops and played small parts in the shows. After the first year, Hanks decided to drop out of college and stay in Cleveland. He stayed for three years. "Working at that theater was paradise," he said. "I loved Cleveland."

During his years with Dowling, Hanks toured Ohio with the theater company. By the end of three years, Hanks knew he wanted to be an actor. In 1978 he was ready to move to New York and look for acting work full time.

BOSOM BUDDIES

Hanks's life changed dramatically in 1978. That year, he married Samantha Lewis and moved to New York. The 22-year-old Hanks knew he had acting skills, but he had no knowledge of show business. He learned that he needed to compile a résumé of his acting jobs. He learned to bring photos of himself to auditions.

Hanks auditioned for every job he heard about. He was picked for a part in the short-lived TV series "Mazes and Monsters." Then he had a role in the slasher movie *He Knows You're Alone*. Through the next two years, Hanks found just enough work to support his wife and his infant son, Colin.

In 1980 Hanks auditioned for a new ABC comedy series called "Bosom Buddies." Writer and producer Chris Thompson was looking for two actors to star in his new sitcom. The show was about two men who need a place to live. They dress up as women so that they can live at an all-women hotel. Thompson had picked Peter Scolari for one of the main roles. When Thompson saw Hanks, he knew he had found his other star.

"Hanks was funnier than anyone else," remembered Thompson. "And that's what I look for when casting a comedy." At the time, Thompson didn't guess that Hanks would become so popular. "You don't put star around his name," he added. "Hanks has a sort of unusual face."

Hanks, meanwhile, was thrilled that he had the part. He loved the opportunity to act—and he liked the steady work. He didn't, however, like the fact that every day on the set he had to dress like a woman. "I had a bad attitude," he admitted about the costumes.

Tom Hanks and Peter Scolari in the hit sitcom, "Bosom Buddies."

Still, the two years of steady acting helped Hanks sharpen his comic skills.

By 1982 ABC canceled the show. Hanks felt exhausted. He wondered what he would be acting in next. He thought he could go back to working in the theater, hanging lights and pulling the curtain. What he didn't know was that someone had been watching his acting career and was ready to make him a star.

SPLASH

When "Bosom Buddies" was canceled, Hanks was just beginning to reveal his talent at playing an average guy. At the same time, director Ron Howard was looking for an average guy to star in his next movie, *Splash*. One of Howard's assistants was a fan of Hanks. The assistant thought Hanks was the right actor for the part. Howard watched Hanks's acting, and he liked what he saw.

Howard asked Hanks to audition for a part in *Splash*. He wanted Hanks to play Allen Bauer, a man who falls in love with a mermaid. Hanks arrived at the audition wearing jeans, a work shirt, and construction boots. At the time, Hanks said he wanted to dress as he felt. He wanted to be casual at the audition. Howard hired him.

Ron Howard was starting to make a name for himself as a director. *Splash*, he hoped, would boost his directing career. Once he had hired Hanks, he hired two more unknown actors to round out the

Tom Hanks starred with Daryl Hannah in the hit movie, "Splash."

Director Ron Howard worked with Hanks on the movie, "Splash." Since the success of that movie, Howard has become one of Hollywood's favorite directors.

cast. Newcomer Daryl Hannah would play Madison, the mermaid. New comic John Candy would play Hanks's loudmouthed brother.

During filming, Hanks received a crash course in movie acting. He was used to the exaggerated style of TV sitcom actors. He was also used to the fast-paced shooting schedule of a weekly show. On several occasions, Howard sat down with Hanks and explained that there were differences between shooting a half-hour show and a full-length feature film. Hanks quickly caught on.

In 1984 *Splash* was released to theaters across the country. Immediately, reporters began writing about Splashmania. Critics called the movie a "dazzler." The movie cost the studio $9 million to create. It earned $60 million at the box office. The careers of Hanks, Hannah, Candy, and Howard took off.

Hanks was amazed at the movie's success. He was starring in his first big film—and it was a raging success. "You can't get it much better, right outta the box," Hanks declared at the time. "It's perfect."

BUILDING A CAREER

Tom Hanks was famous, but he also wanted to keep acting. Scripts started to pile into his office. Hanks accepted all the offers that he could.
In 1984 he worked on four movies. *Bachelor Party*, *The Man With*

One Red Shoe, *Volunteers*, and *The Money Pit* were made quickly. None matched the box office success of *Splash*. None, the critics said, were blockbusters. Some people criticized Hanks for choosing to act in these movies. But he defended himself. "This is what I do," he explained at the time. "I'm an actor. An actor has to act. What else am I supposed to do—sit around the house?"

Tom Hanks and John Candy in the movie, "Volunteers."

As the four movie projects ended, more people wanted Hanks to read their scripts and star in their movies. Hanks hired a personal manager and an agent to read through the manuscripts that arrived in the mail—sometimes he received 20 a day. His manager and agent sent Hanks the best scripts. Hanks read about three a day.

Of all these scripts, the one for the movie *Nothing in Common* stood out. The script was about David Basner, a fast-talking executive. Basner's smooth life is interrupted when his parents tell him they are divorcing. Veteran actor Jackie Gleason was chosen for the part of Basner's father.

"You know in the first three pages if you're going to want to do the thing or not," said Hanks. "With this script it was clear that this was going to be a good movie." He accepted the script and began working on the rewrites.

Hanks thinks of *Nothing in Common* as a turning point in his career because he was involved in the project from the beginning. During the eight months of rewriting, Hanks worked with the producer to create a good script.

When filming began, Hanks watched Gleason and learned much about the business from the experienced actor. He learned not to make excuses for anything. He learned not to assign blame or show remorse. If something went wrong, Hanks saw that Gleason took the blame if it was Gleason's fault.

Jackie Gleason considered Hanks a fine actor.

For his part, Gleason was impressed with the young actor. After filming, Gleason stated, "He moves like a funny guy. The verdict on Tom Hanks is that he's got it."

LIFE CHANGES

During the filming of *Nothing in Common*, Hanks divorced his wife. By this time, he had two children; his son was six years old and his daughter was one. Custody of the children went to Samantha.

During the divorce, Hanks kept to himself and rarely talked to reporters about his family. He stayed close to a group of friends he had known for years. Many of these friends weren't even in the movie business.

"Tom is what I call the hat pack," said one friend. "You know, a bunch of guys who occasionally wear hats, and that's about as wild as they ever get."

To keep busy, Hanks kept accepting movie roles, and he kept acting. In 1986 he starred in two more movies. In *Every Time We Say Good-Bye*, Hanks played a World War II fighter pilot who falls in love with an Israeli girl. The critics disliked the movie and said that Hanks had made an unfunny flop.

Hanks kept working. His next role was as Pep Streebek, a wise-cracking detective, in *Dragnet*. By now, Hanks had played almost every kind of comic role. "I do this thing fairly well," insisted Hanks about his movie roles. "I'm a funny guy. I guess that's the thing I am. I'm not afraid to admit that. . .I like being a funny guy." His role in *Nothing in Common*, however, was still his favorite. That role showed Hanks that he could act in more serious roles.

By 1986 Hanks had been in the movie industry six years and had made nine movies. He still, however, could walk down the street without being recognized. One time, he walked in New York City without wearing a pair of sunglasses. No one recognized him. "I guess I have that quality of being a bit like everyone else," he said.

MORE BIG BREAKS

In 1987 Hanks worked on the set of *Big*, a movie about Josh Baskin, a 12-year-old boy who makes a wish to be bigger. Hanks played the boy once he becomes older. The role was a challenge for 31-year-old Hanks. He had to act like a 12-year-old who suddenly has a larger body.

"What I dug about this movie," recalled Hanks, "was there was no car chase, no bad guys, no guns. A massive amount of the movie is just two people sitting around talking."

To become a 12-year-old, Hanks studied David Moscow, the actor who played the young Josh. Hanks watched how Moscow laughed and walked. He listened to the phrases Moscow and his friends used. Hanks also recalled memories from his own childhood in junior high. The hardest part of playing a young boy, said Hanks, was regaining a kid's sense of play.

In the movie, once Josh becomes an adult, his friend helps him to get a job at a toy company. The president is so impressed with Josh that he promotes Josh to vice president in charge of development. Josh's job is to sit in an office and play with toys. In one scene the president of the toy company and Hanks's character meet in a toy store. They dance a duet on giant piano keys embedded in the store's floor. "That scene was exhausting," remembered Hanks. "It was like jumping rope for ten hours."

When the film was complete, a special screening of the movie was arranged. A test audience was asked to watch *Big* and tell the studio what they liked and disliked about it. Hanks went to that screening, too. He didn't want to be recognized so he wore a baseball cap across his forehead. As he watched himself on screen, he kept a straight face and never laughed at his own jokes. The audience, however, laughed and laughed. They loved it.

This scene in "Big" made Hanks a household name.

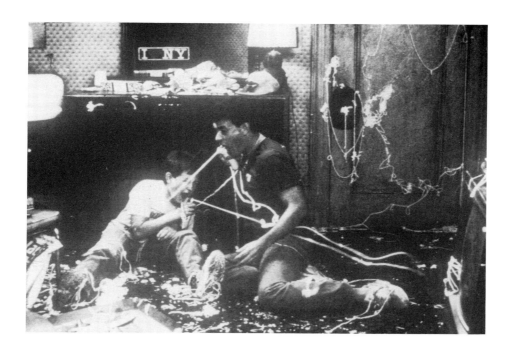

Hanks playing a 12-year-old boy in a grown man's body in the movie, "Big."

After the screening, Hanks talked to reporters about his role. "*Big* was probably my purest, the least fake performance," he said.

After a five-month break, Hanks began work on his next movie *The 'Burbs*. In that movie, Hanks played a homeowner who is suspicious about what his new neighbors are up to.

While he was filming *The 'Burbs*, *Big* was playing in theaters and became a hit. Critics once again praised Hanks. After less-than-great performances, they wrote, Hanks had once again proved he was a great actor. The real praise came when he was nominated for an Academy Award for his work in *Big*. "Yes," admitted Hanks, "being nominated was a *nice* thing."

Although he didn't win the award, Hanks was almost too busy to notice. He had finished working on *The 'Burbs* and was well into making his eleventh movie, *Punchline*.

In *Punchline*, as in *Nothing in Common*, Hanks played a more serious and emotional role. He starred as Steven Gold, an unsuccessful medical student who wants to be a stand-up comic. To prepare for his role, Hanks worked at real comedy clubs in front of live audiences. He worked hard to play the angry and tormented comic.

In the move, the troubled Steven tutors a New Jersey housewife who also dreams of working in comedy clubs. Sally Field played that part. "Tom is very entertaining and funny and easy to be around," said Field about her costar. "But you know there's a sad side, a dark side. And that's what makes him so compelling on the screen."

"I think *Punchline* has more of my emotion in it [than any other movie]," revealed Hanks.

SLOWING DOWN AND GETTING MARRIED

Once again, Hanks had worked nonstop for over a year. The scripts kept coming in and Hanks kept saying yes to acting jobs. Just as in 1984, Hanks didn't want to sit around and worry about his next movie role. "I had a great desire to be working," Hanks admitted. "You do get these feelings that you're never ever going to work again."

When a reporter asked Hanks why he worked so much, Hanks just shrugged. He explained that he worked in so many movies because there was so much he wanted to learn and figure out.

Hanks began to choose his roles more carefully that he had in his earlier career. He looked for movies that had some variety in them. He looked for ones that would be filmed on location and not just in a California studio. He knows that not all his movies have been popular, but, he said, "I've never done the same thing twice. And how many people can say that? Some [movies] have bombed, but who cares?"

After filming the last four movies—*Big*, *Dragnet*, *The 'Burbs*, and *Punchline*—Hanks was exhausted. He was so worn out that he caught pneumonia. He spent a month recovering from the illness.

Hanks knew that this time he had been working too hard. He decided not to work at all in 1988. Other things started to become more important to him—namely his children and his new girlfriend, Rita Wilson.

Since Hanks's divorce in 1985, his son and daughter had lived with their mother in northern California. Whenever he could, Hanks visited them. He also spent more and more time with Wilson. The two had met on the set of *Volunteers* about three years before. In that movie, Wilson played the woman who falls in love with Hanks's character.

In April 1988 Hanks and Wilson were married. In one interview before the wedding, Hanks described why he thought that this marriage would last. "We have laughed an awful lot," he explained. "You need that. The person you're gonna marry is somebody you're gonna probably talk to for the rest of your life. You're gonna have to want to laugh."

With all his success, Hanks still had the same friends. He still drove the same van. He still wore blue jeans. After a year of rest, Hanks was ready to continue his rising career.

MORE HITS AND MISSES

"I don't know if it's possible to have a specific approach [to comedy]," Hanks told a reporter. "I don't have a system or even think about [being funny] very much. Something happens."

Fresh from his vacation, Hanks's next three movie roles were different and fit into his quirky style. *Turner and Hooch*, which appeared in theaters in 1989, was different because of the costar. In this movie, Hanks played a police detective whose life is changed by a large, drooling dog. Hanks wanted to do this film simply because he'd get to work with a dog.

Shortly afterward, Hanks played Joe Banks in *Joe Versus the Volcano*. In this comedy, Hanks played a depressed worker who thinks he is dying. Joe's life turns upside down when he agrees to jump into a volcano to save an island and its people.

It wasn't long before Hanks began working on *Bonfire of the Vanities*. In *Bonfire*, Hanks played a rich man who is a passenger in a car that accidentally hits and kills a young man. Hanks's character spends the rest of the movie trying to hide the murder. Once again critics were not impressed with Hanks's performance.

After *Bonfire*, Hanks took another break—he didn't want to risk getting sick again. "It was the best thing for everybody," remembered Hanks. "I needed a break from the industry."

Hanks and Melanie Griffith in "Bonfire of the Vanities."

Hanks spent his vacation enjoying his favorite hobby—surfing. Hanks tried to explain why he loved surfing so much. He said that surfers get scared. The waves can throw surfers underwater. Sometimes they can't fight them. "You have to learn to be comfortable down there," he said. "It's a good life experience."

Because he couldn't surf forever, Hanks accepted another movie role in 1991. In *A League of Their Own*, he played a down-and-out baseball player who manages a team of women players. He picked this film because, for a while, he wanted to get away from being thought of as a nice, cute, average actor.

When director Penny Marshall told Hanks that he could have the role, she said she did not want him to be cute. "Believe me," Hanks told Marshall, "I don't want to be cute."

The movie did well in the box office, and Hanks was ready to work on something new. He had already said yes to two more movies: the romantic comedy *Sleepless in Seattle* and the drama *Philadelphia*.

ANOTHER TURNING POINT

The public first saw *Sleepless in Seattle*, Hanks's seventeenth movie, in 1993. In the film, Hanks played Sam Balwin, a widower living in Seattle with his young son. The son calls into a radio talk show and the whole country hears about Sam's loss and his son's wish for them to be happy again.

Hanks described why he chose to star in this movie. "It was truly great," he said, "not to be playing a guy who has some kooky thing happen to him." The fun and romance of the movie made it a hit at the box office.

In *Philadelphia*, however, Hanks was asked to call up different, more serious emotions. He was asked to play a successful lawyer who is fired from his job when his boss finds out he has AIDS.

When he read the script, Hanks knew he wanted to be a part of the project. He felt that the movie was powerful. "It is a very real approach to what is going on [with this illness]," he explained.

Hanks in the hit movie of 1993, "Sleepless in Seattle."

Hanks played an AIDS victim in the controversial hit movie of 1994, "Philadelphia."

In the movie, the AIDS virus takes a toll on Hanks's character and makes him weaker and weaker. For the role, Hanks lost 30 pounds and had his hair thinned.

When TriStar studio decided to make *Philadelphia*, the executives knew the movie covered delicate subjects. Homosexuality, AIDS, and people's fear of the virus were all part of the movie. The studio hoped that Hanks's charm and likeability would help audiences accept this film.

At the 1994 Academy Awards, Hanks won an Oscar for Best Actor. The movie's title song, "Streets of Philadelphia," won an Oscar for best original song. Hanks and the movie's cast and crew had won over audiences.

With all the publicity surrounding his Academy Award, more and more reporters wanted to interview Hanks. Although he talked about his movie roles, he kept quiet about his personal life. Hanks never allowed a reporter into his home. Whenever he was interviewed, Hanks met the writer either in his office or at a restaurant. He didn't talk about personal details. Part of the reason was that Hanks's children were growing up. His son from his first marriage was now 15 years old and his daughter was ten. Hanks and Wilson also had a son, Chester, who was three. Hanks wanted to protect them from publicity.

Tom Hanks accepting the Academy Award for Best Actor in "Philadelphia."

Hanks believes he is a private person because of the moving around he did when he was young. He once explained that he never had many friends. If he started to make a friend, his family would move. Hanks would say good-bye, and he'd have to start making friends again in a new city and new school. "I don't think it's part of my mental makeup to completely open myself up to people I know," he admitted.

One of Hanks's surfing buddies summed up Hanks's behavior. He said Hanks was an intense, complex person, but that he never let his real self show.

NO SET PLANS FOR THE FUTURE

In 1989 a reporter asked Hanks if he had a grand plan for the next couple of years. Hanks replied that he had no plans at all. He knew of actors who constantly plan their careers and, he added, it simply doesn't work.

A few years later when the subject of future plans came up again, Hanks's answer was still the same. "I just try never to worry," he said, confidently. "Why worry when you can wing it?"

Hanks did admit to one future plan. He said that he would one day like to direct movies. He's had some experience working behind the camera. In 1993 he directed a segment of the TV show "Fallen Angels." The series included six mystery stories. Hanks directed the story titled "I'll Be Waiting."

That same year, he directed an episode of the TV series "A League of Their Own." He's not sure if he'll be directing more in the future. But he'd certainly like the chance to be behind the scenes again.

Whether the future holds more comedy and drama roles or a new role as director, Hanks will certainly stay a popular person in Hollywood. He's secure in his career, yet he's still the same down-to-earth guy his friends admire.

"What are you going to do?" Hanks asks about his fame and fortune. "Who can explain any of this? I mean, it's just *movies* that we're talking about."

TV SHOWS AND MOVIES (1978-1993)

1978	Mazes and Monsters (TV show)
1980	He Knows You're Alone
1980-1982	Bosom Buddies (TV show)
1984	Splash
1984	Bachelor Party
1985	The Man With One Red Shoe
1985	Volunteers
1986	The Money Pit
1986	Nothing in Common
1986	Every Time We Say Good-Bye
1987	Dragnet
1988	Big
1988	Punchline
1989	The 'Burbs
1989	Turner and Hooch
1990	Joe Versus the Volcano
1990	Bonfire of the Vanities
1992	Tales from the Crypt: None but the Lonely Heart (TV show)
1992	A League of Their Own
1993	Sleepless in Seattle
1993	Fallen Angels (directing; TV show)
1993	A League of Their Own (directing; TV show)
1993	Philadelphia

TOM HANKS'S ADDRESS

To send a letter to Tom Hanks, write to:

Tom Hanks
321 S. Anita Avenue
Los Angeles, CA 90049

If you want to receive a reply, enclose a self-addressed stamped envelope (SASE) with your letter.